ACHIEVING FULFILLMENT

10 Simple Strategies

Placing You On The Path To

Peace

Donna Cooper

Donna Cooper

They are who they are
You can not make them
 into someone else

Let them become what they want

Help them be themselves.

If you can, then ok
If not, move on

R.A.M.M.

Copyright c 2015 Donna Cooper

PREFACE

As an African-American, wait, I prefer black. It's quicker. As a black working actress living in New York back from twenty years in Hollywood I've met my share of unhappy people, and not just actors. My non-fiction humorous self-help book 'Achieving Fulfillment: 10 Simple Strategies Placing You On The Path To Peace' weaves together comical real life antics with chapters called 'links' that give practical guidelines to help steer you towards a hopefully happier life experience. There are ten links in all.

I am fortunate to have worked as a stand up comic, shot television shows, movies and loads of commercials (See me threaten a scapegoat in a GEICO spot), traveled around the world, golfed in Hawai'i and married an adorable Federal agent. Conversely, I have also suffered from child abuse, addiction, sexual assault, parental death as a child, poverty, familial mental illness, and systemic cancer. These issues and then some affect many of us if not all of us. This book tells you about my old unfortunate ways of dealing with life that may seem outlandish at times, but everything I discuss has happened to me. These ten links are practical attainable solutions dealing honestly with life while having a laugh at my ridiculousness.

These solutions have allowed me to find peace when by all counts I should have been bedridden with severe depression.

The anecdotes are all true.

This book is not only meant to entertain you, but to improve some or all of your life. That is the hopeful out come of this fun self help guide.

INTRODUCTION

The practical advice I've given and received throughout the years has all been put to the test. Working as a stand-up comic and actress in NY and LA, losing friends and lovers through death or by choice, experiencing the death of a parent and nursing the other back to health, surviving childhood sexual abuse, living with cancer, enjoying the ups and downs of marriage, which happens to be an interracial one, and the continued work successes as well as ongoing family drama, paying bills, and the humdrum cycle of life are all part of my living experience that at one time or another has given me angst and sleepless nights.

Having survived and then thrived throughout years of very high highs and very low lows I am grateful for the advice and the books I've read that kept me moving forward. I was fortunate enough to marry a man that through his own journey; many years of high level government experience in law enforcement, has helped broaden my views. His extensive psychological knowledge has been invaluable. Our belief that life is to be enjoyed not endured is the catalyst for penning this book. The pool of ideas, life experiences and solutions tried and true are finely honed and shared for all to benefit if they so choose.

"Achieving Fulfillment" is about gaining peace in your life. It is about being happy. We each have our own definition of what brings us peace or what makes us happy. Conversely, there are a number of concepts we would all agree on that can make a person miserable. Reading "Achieving Fulfillment" will guide you away from the habits, thoughts, and unconscious behavior that doesn't serve you. You have this one life. Let this book be your guide to making it better. It is all about you.

Experience has shown me that true contentment usually involves some form of acceptance. Accepting a situation, person, place, thing as it is truly allows us to move in a direction that will ultimately bring us closer to achieving our personal goals of fulfillment; being happy. You don't have to like the situation. Accept it as it is in order to move on to better, calmer, nicer and every other adjective that makes you feel good.

These ideas are presented to you in ten separate sections or "links". They will help you face life: past, present and future. These links stand alone but do build on one another so reading them in order is recommended. Each link helps you to build your chain. Each link moves you closer to attaining a feeling of contentment. They might sound familiar. Many have certainly been touched upon on talk shows. Some of them may remind you of sage advice from a grandmother or from an old friend. You may have stumbled on some of these ideas in a magazine or textbook years ago but have since forgotten them or the clippings are torn and now illegible.

Years of working in the entertainment industry has taught me a lot. Navigating a career in front of the camera with no obvious corporate ladder to climb takes patience, discipline, insight and a tough skin. Supporting myself through the lean years, and the not so lean years financially and emotionally has lead me to face my past, my fears and ultimately my reality.

Although there truly are no real shortcuts in life, "Achieving Fulfillment" can guide you to a better understanding of yourself and how to live a happier life. "Achieving Fulfillment" offers practical attainable solutions dealing honestly with life. These solutions have allowed me to find peace when by all counts I should have been bedridden with severe depression. Facing life head on sounds aggressive and tough. Actually, you will find that it is calming and freeing. Keep reading and you will find out for yourself.

This book offers the reader a game plan. Each section of this book is actually a link in the chain of your happiness. When you have a complete chain, watch your world open up. The reality is you have this one life today to live. Why not make each day as wonderful and as memorable as you possibly can? Whatever your situation, if you follow these well thought out suggestions, you can finally live the life you want. Live the life you deserve.

It is time to achieve fulfillment. You are supported in this endeavor. I applaud you for taking the first step toward your fulfillment. Thank you for reading this book and making your own chain of joy. Enjoy it. The book and your life.

CONTENTS

First Link: Live In The Present	15
Second Link: Accept Things As They Are	24
Third Link: Complainig Is Not For You	34
Fourth Link: Speak Up When Something Is Wrong	40
Fifth Link: Live Fearlessly	48
Sixth Link: Take Care Of Basics	61
Seventh Link: Control Yourself	71
Eighth Link: Stop Doing What Is Not Working	79
Ninth Link: Believe In Something Greater Than Yourself	84
Tenth Link: Surrender Equals Peace	90
CONCLUSION	94

Donna Cooper

KNOW YOUR LINKS

First Link
Live In The Present

Second Link
Accept Things As They Are

Third Link
Complaining Is Not For You

Fourth Link
Speak Up When Something Is Wrong

Fifth Link
Live Fearlessly

Sixth Link
Take Care Of The Basics

Seventh Link
Control Yourself

Eighth Link
Stop Doing What Is Not Working

Ninth Link
Believe In Something Greater Than Yourself

Tenth Link
Surrender Equals Peace

FIRST LINK

Live In The Present

UNLINKED:

In the spring of 1991 I left New York City to entertain the troops as a stand-up comic on a cruise ship for two weeks in the Middle East. Bahrain to be exact. I stayed for a year. This story takes place about a month before I returned to the states. Sitting on a bus into downtown Rotana in Bahrain I complained to a new found friend about my past relationships with men. I spoke freely.

On the bus ride back, I picked up where I left off and continued to air my negative man views and to hang out my dirty laundry.
That night on the cruise ship I was wishing well a number of soldiers who were being deployed early that next day. One gentleman in the Air Force caught my attention. He was handsome with a warm smile. His athletic build attracted me and listening to him speak, his intelligence drew me in. He also looked familiar. I

wanted to at least introduce myself and say 'goodbye'.

SOLDIER: I know you are the comic performing on the cruise ship. I think you're pretty funny. And pretty, and just well, hot, and I wanted to ask you out.
DONNA: Why didn't you?
SOLDIER: Well, I was on the bus the other day heading downtown. You seemed so miserable and fed up with men, I figured you wouldn't want to talk to me.
DONNA: I would definitely have talked to you. So you didn't have the confidence to come over and talk?
SOLDIER: Honestly? You were so stuck in your past I didn't know if you could enjoy the present. And basically, that's all I've got.

(Actual conversation had in 1991 when I entertained the troops aboard a cruise ship docked in the Persian Gulf)

LINK:

Are you constantly replaying things that happened to you in the past? Reliving old hurts, past mistakes done to you and by you? Life changing chances that were let go out of fear?

Or in contrast, do you spend the rest of your time ruminating about the unknown future fretting about what may be, might, could happen? Running scenarios over and over with the 'what if...' caption attached? Hoping that you can manipulate the outcome of all you do?

Are you grounded in the here and now?
It sounds silly to say live in the present. This is not science fiction, no teleporters in sight, so where else would you be? Physically you are here now, but unfortunately most of us are either wallowing in the past or worrying about the future.

Right now your body is sitting, laying down or standing holding this book and reading. You are focusing on the words and taking them in; agreeing, disagreeing, understanding or not quite getting it. You are solidly in the present. A thought or two may jump into your head as you read, 'what to make for dinner?', 'oh, I need to call such and such back', but you gently guide your thoughts back and remain in the present.

One of the great things about reading is your focus is primarily only in the here and now. You are not pondering on what you did or didn't get done yesterday. The missed opportunities and bad breaks are not taunting you while you read. (Ok, granted because I brought them up they are now in your head but you smile, push them out and return to living in the present.) When you are not reading, living in the present takes practice.

Living fully in each moment is tough. Grounding yourself with breathing can help. Check in with your breathing during the day.

Obviously you are breathing or else you couldn't check in with it, but how are you breathing? Are your breaths quick and shallow? Are you barely breathing and then gulping small gasps unevenly? Or are you barely breathing then taking in long exasperated lumbered pants?

Dive into your own rhythm. Pay attention to what makes you light headed or what makes you calm. Close your mouth and breathe in through your nose and out of a relaxed mouth. Do this all day, every hour, before breakfast, after lunch, while driving, right before bed, before kissing, while watching television, checking email and any other time you can think of to help keep you present. It will help you stay in the moment where you belong, mind and body together.

Focusing on the tasks at hand will also help ground you in the present. A busy day at work or running errands flies by because you are fully engaged in each moment even if part of you is playing beat the clock. Notice how different you are when you are playing beat the clock working on a deadline. You are hyper focused and in the zone. No room for idle chit chat during those times. The task at hand has all your attention. Try that without the anxiety attached. Live life that way.

Time goes by no matter what you do. Vexing about the future doesn't keep it from coming. Longing for the past doesn't bring it back. Getting ready in the morning can take on a new life as you turn all your attention to the present. Dining (or shoveling in breakfast) changes when you actually focus on tasting each morsel of food.

This isn't about slowing down, which actually isn't a bad idea; it is about being fully engaged in your life.

Some of you will have trouble appreciating your present because of a traumatic past. Physical and mental abuse, not being cared for the way you needed to be qualifies as trauma; but only you can identify the things in your past that color your present and keep you from being your authentic you. The authentic you is meant to be happy, not skipping down the street singing everyday, but experiencing each day feeling love and contentment in your own skin.

Issues from childhood, early teens or adulthood that are hurtful can infect your perception of yourself, your self worth, decision making, and complicate your relationships leaving you feeling less than, lonely and even depressed. If any of this sounds familiar it is absolutely necessary you do something about it. To live in the present you have to let go of the past.

Psychiatrists, psychologists and therapists are fantastic resources. If you EVER have the opportunity to speak with one of these individuals, DO IT. Please remember that these people are resources, guides to help you stand on your own two feet and continue to make your life your own. They are not a substitute for negligent, unstable parents or abusive girlfriends.

Remember that you have the power to be happy. Don't give it away.

Living in the present is the first step to being happy. It is tough to be happy when you are burdened daily with dark, scarring, harmful secrets of the past. For some, therapy is not an option, but you must opt to remove the infections of your past if you plan on being happy.

Get a notebook. Some would call it a journal, but that can seem too precious. Yes, a lovely leather bound key lock tome would be lovely, but a $1.50 notebook from the grocery store works just as well. You want to get healthy and get into the present not give Hemingway or Sylvia Plath a run for their money. You want to start purging the trauma, get rid of the ghosts and scars of the past. Write them down in specific detail. Try to do this when you have time alone to feel the feelings that will come up. Make sure you have the time to cry, get angry, write more then perhaps nap. Write some more. This could take many weekends, many nights, months even years as you take the time to release all that you have kept stored.

If you are in a loving relationship you might want to share what you are doing but not the work itself. This is only work you can do. No one else. Your alone time is vital. If you do not feel safe in your present relationship, take your alone time as you can and know you need to do this for yourself.

Fill the notebook with all the hurts you have experienced. It might take a few notebooks. Get it out. Be specific. Now be object-ive, as you can. What advice would you give someone if they read to you what you have just written? How would you suggest they help themselves?

Achieving Fulfillment

Then do it. Eventually you will throw away the notebooks. Or shred them. Or burn them. Get rid of them. What is done is done and it can not be changed.

Be present for yourself unencumbered by events of the past.

After your purge, this may be the only time to compare yourself to others to get some perspective on your life. Unfortunately, in this world as some may be better off than you, there are also those that have had it worse.

Misery loves company. Listening to someone else's misery can help you within reason . Your father was perhaps an aloof cold man that provided for you but never said, "I love you." Your co-worker's father traded her for crack. Keep things in perspective. Your hurts and needs are your own. As you absolve yourself of the heinous things in your past try to remember that someone out there has had it worse and they have survived, some even thrived.

Working with a qualified person is optimum, but don't settle for darkness if you won't go that route. Writing things down can save your sanity and bring you back to the present. You may even have a friend you prefer to speak to as well as the writing. Please make sure the friend is a trusted one who hates to gossip and knows their part is really just to listen not take up a crusade to expose the uncle that abused you. Trust your notebook first.

Your spouse, your children, your friends maybe even your boss and co-workers will appreciate having ALL of you present. They don't want you lost reliving the past good or bad. They don't want to be punished for things they didn't do simply because you carry the vengeance of a angry hurt child. Start being fair to them and to yourself.

Worrying and stressing about the future also takes away from your life in the here and now. It cripples you. Stressing about things yet to come, or that have yet to happen (and probably won't) erodes your ability to make good decisions about the future. Use what you have learned to stay in the now. Obviously you make plans for the future (saving accounts, 401k's, retirement funds, vacations, yearly check ups, dinner and a movie this weekend) but it is the obsessing about them that does the damage.

Some spend so much time worrying about an event, or date or meeting that when the time comes their performance is lackluster and they are too exhausted to appreciate the event. Ever happen to you? You are like the child at Christmas who is so overly excited about the Santa visit that once the magic day arrives they are usually barely able to keep their eyes open and fall asleep amongst the discarded wrapping paper. Of course it is a wonderful part of life being excited especially about a positive event, but as adults the negative part of being excited can rear its head as worry and that takes us firmly out of the present.

You can not go into the future to make it turn out as we would like. What you can do is make your right now as stellar as you can. You want money for a vacation next year, so think: do I really need to buy a cup of coffee and sweet treat everyday?

Positive present action taken today allows tomorrow to be great. If you have purged your past perhaps you can muscle through without the comfort of a flourless chocolate cookie today. You save money for your holiday. You aren't comforting old hurts and hey you might even drop a pound or two.

Your present is where the action is.

Achieving Fulfillment

You will be surprised how wonderful your future will be if you consciously pursue the title of this chapter.

Since we can not control life we have no idea what will come our way. Life involves disappointment, mistakes, tragedy, sickness as well as the positives. Do the best you can to stay present. As the negatives come up we are better able to cope if we have done the hard work on ourselves. Ground yourself in the knowledge that your life has meaning, that you are necessary and relevant or you wouldn't be here. You are an integral part of the puzzle.

Your future largely reflects your loving grounded choices you make in the present.

Here's to TODAY.

It's been said old people live in the past, young people live in the future, and a wise person lives in the present. Give yourself a break. Forgive yourself and others. Everyone makes mistakes. Everyone has failed in some way. Bring yourself back to the present. Remember, if you do not celebrate the delicacy of each moment, each day, you have certainly lost something you can never get back.

SECOND LINK

Accept Things As They Are

UNLINKED:

As a high school senior I took a Greyhound bus from Long Island, NY to visit my older brother in college in Massachusetts. At the time the bus made a few stops before pulling into downtown Boston. One of those stops was called Riverside. Remember, this is long ago and far away before cell phones, laptops and anything else that facilitates communication and information for fun and safe travel. That is where the story begins.

After visiting my brother and feeling very grown-up I took the 'T', Massachusetts mass transit system, to Riverside station and purchased my ticket back to NY from the less than friendly Greyhound employee. I asked when my bus would arrive and he said any minute. Deciding on a machine snack, a bus pulls in.

"New York City. All board for the bus to New York City."

I grabbed my small overstuffed cream colored canvas duffle bag and my oversized pleather pocketbook and headed outside.

"New York, Miss?"
"Yes."
"Come on up and grab a seat"

And I did. The driver said he would collect the tickets after the next two stops. Fine with me. I was looking forward to eating the half of a hoagie I had saved from the night before and jumping back into my latest W. Somerset Maugham novel.

The bus made a couple of stops before we headed through the then physical toll plaza and onto the Mass Pike heading south. The Mass Pike is a very busy main highway. Five lanes in each direction with a minimum speed of 75 mph. These days, I believe the speed limit is 105 in the slow lane.

Roaring down the highway, I feel there is something amiss. The last woman to get on the bus clearly said, "New York City?" when she boarded and the driver clearly said "yes". I needed to be on Long Island. NYC is definitely not Long Island. Granted they are only separated by the East River but in reality they are worlds apart. A teenager with a highly emotional, stressed widowed mother who is barely keeping it together daily can not be dropped off in NYC when said mother is waiting at the station on Long Island. I approach the driver.

"Uh, are you going to Long Island?"
"Nope. New York City. The bus says New York City. "
"So you couldn't just drop me at the station on Long Island?"
"No. Please sit down."

"Are you sure"
"The bus that goes to Long Island says 'Long Island' on it"
"Well, I have to get off. My mother is expecting me at the bus station on Long Island. Please pull over."
"We're on the Mass Pike!"
"So? I need to ge off and get back to the Riverside station so I can get on the bus to Long Island…"
"I can not pull over on the Mass Pike.."

I honestly don't remember what I said after that but what I do remember is the driver pulled over and let me out on the Massachusetts Turnpike. I stood on a grassy divider, the only safe haven from the ten lanes of traffic. Five in each direction.

Grateful to have the chance to catch the actual bus home I never once thought about the dangerous reality of my situation. I knew I needed to make my way back to the bus station where I got on. Never receiving a badge for compass reading in Girls Scouts I was completely lost. I somehow figured out that I needed to cross the five lanes heading away from the direction that my old bus ride had been taking me in order to get back to the Riverside bus station. Crossing highway traffic wasn't the only obstacle. There was a chain link fence topped with barbed wire keeping me from stepping into traffic.

Without hesitation I flung my pocketbook and duffel bag over the fence. Luckily they landed on the median. I did lose a pair of dirty underwear and a t-shirt shoved in at the top of the duffel bag into oncoming traffic, but that was the least of my worries. I knew if my goods went first I would have to follow. And follow I did. I threw myself onto that fence without hesitation.

Unfortunately the fence was not made for climbing.

The fence bowed and sagged as I climbed. I was inches from the tops of the furious, honking, unsympathetic motorists whizzing by. I kept climbing.

When I reached the barbed wire I sucked it up, grabbed hold, pulled my 17 year old body up and then flung myself to the otherside. See? Easy peasy. I quickly gathered my ragtag belongings and looked to cross the five lanes of traffic.

Keeping my eye on the traffic, I knew if I could get across I could scurry up the embankment and find my way back to the bus station. Sheer will and determination got me safely across. I was not going to miss my bus!

Miraculously, I found the bus station and ran in. The jaded ticket clerk looked as if he had seen a ghost as I approached the window panting and gasping for air.

"Did. The. Long Island...bus come?"
"Uh. No. Uh Didn't you...uh..the bus to Long Island just pulled in..."
"Oh. Thanks"

Without missing a beat I turned and walked out to the bus.

"Sir. Does this bus go to Long Island?"
"Yup. See? Says 'Long Island' right up front."
"Here's my ticket."
"Thanks Miss. Have a nice ride!"

And I did. Wishing and hoping and wanting things to be different makes life tough.

Acceptance is key.

LINK:

Accepting people, places, and things as they are is the next link in your chain. What is important to remember is that the word 'accept' is not synonymous with the word 'like'. Accepting that your boyfriend prefers to spend time with your new friend from work is essential to your happiness. You don't like it, but by accepting the reality of the situation you can stop wasting time with your soon to be ex and focus on people that appreciate you. This isn't just sound dating advice, it works for all aspects of life.

The world is not put together just to annoy you, though some of you may beg to differ. The way some people drive oblivious to others and the rules of the road is appalling. Or you politely let someone pull out in front of you and they are driving so slowly you feel like you are driving backwards is enough to make you scream, "JUST GO!" (or is that just me?) The way some folks seem to have been raised by a pack of wolves, where the phrases 'excuse me', 'thank you' and 'please' don't exist. Or the crazy bunch that must always speak loudly on their cell phones in a crowded place or texting while walking or driving.(callback here to driving angst). These are but a modicum of ways folks can drive you insane. You are muttering and sputtering to yourself in the grocery store about how rude folks are these days because you can barely get past the women whose shopping cart and unruly offspring are taking up the aisle and she is nowhere to be found. (FYI, she is at work. They are with the grandmother who is weeping quietly hiding in the bakery section).

There are rules and laws and the proverbial red tape that make you wish you could make the world according to _____. (Insert your name here.) The common sense that isn't so common has long been an understatement. Why can't things work the way you want them to? Why can't people show up and behave? Do you really have every size except for mine? From paying taxes to putting up with people that disagree with you and jumping through hoops at the job when you know an easier better way, how can you even think about being happy or fulfilled?

You do not have the power to change people, places or things. You do have the power to go in the other direction; to accept them. Remember accepting doesn't involve liking, it involves you releasing your emotional involvement. If you like something you are happy. If you don't like something, it makes you unhappy. Take the emotion out of it, or at least begin to try. Taking out the personal attachment, keeps your blood pressure down and your head from falling off. Interestingly enough, in your acceptance, change occurs.

As you accept things, YOU change. Perhaps you don't want to change. Then maybe you can pass this book onto your niece, brother, neighbor or postman so they can deal with you. (Just kidding. About the dealing with you. Please by all means pass the book around and around.)

Seriously, by accepting the reality you find a way in your comfort zone to continue on in the situation or turn and abandon the event, relationship, or happening. Accept that the place with the great sweet potato fries and homemade coleslaw has uncomfortable seats. Instead of seeing this as a personal attack on your sciatica spearheaded by a cheap owner; bring a cushion to sit on and enjoy yourself.

There is wisdom that can only be tapped in acceptance. You get to make choices when you face reality. Choices that usually leave you feeling empowered.

You live in a crappy place. First clean it. Then decorate to the best of your ability and fix that place up so it (may) start to mirror what you have in your heart. You will feel better about coming home, your general attitude will be better, you smile more, you start getting better tips at work or your superiors recognize your new zest for life, you perform better at work winning a raise or a bonus, pretty soon you either have what you need to move or you can make the major changes to your home you have always wanted.

Yes this is hypothetical, but can you see how accepting what you have can turn into eventually liking it or having the means to better yourself? Can you see how you are much more fun to be around accepting and playing the cards you have in your hand right now? Accepting means you get to enjoy the ride your way.

There is a family friend who truly knows how to enjoy himself. He is retired and likes to be comfortable. When he is invited over for a party he is dressed impeccably and always brings his slippers. Instead of becoming a grouchy homebody, he accepts his need for comfort and acts accordingly. What a smart choice. He has accepted his reality. Hopefully, you will find small ways at first to give over to what is and stop having a tantrum over what is not.

Achieving Fulfillment

You have a friend that never calls. They never invite you over. They never initiate any kind of get together. I mean not ever. If you are happy with always being the one to call and make plans then you have a perfect symbiotic relationship. If you prefer a bit more give and take in your relationships then this person is not a very good friendship candidate for you. If you find yourself in this relationship always asking why they don't call, wishing and hoping they ask about your life you will spend a lot of time feeling a sense of apprehension and uneasiness. Once you accept this person as they are; you stop trying to make them do something they are not going to do. You accept them and then you get to make some choices.

Stop calling? Call if you like with no strings attached? Spend your time with people who are genuinely concerned about your well being? You get to decide. You know what they are about so you release them and yourself from unrealistic expectations. You can still remain friends; see it for what it is, not a very good friendship, but she might give killer baked goods on your birthday! Accept and there will be no angst.

When you see things as they are you don't waste time hoping, and wishing people will do things they are never going to do.

Accepting things as they are doesn't mean you are a boring lemming who does not make waves. It means you are not wasting your precious time and energy trying to do the impossible. Yelling "Go!" at the car in front of you does not make them go. Enjoying meditative classical music or an old school group on the radio doesn't make them go either, yet one of these two things helps you to stay present without shaving a few years off your life or eroding your system by flooding it with too much adrenaline. Chapter one reminds you that the only way to help yourself have a great future is to do your best to have a great present. This applies here. Accepting people and situations as they are, grounds you in the present. This is the reality; embrace it.

Then watch it change. Change is buried deep inside genuine acceptance.

It is also good to remind yourself that everyone in life has a different agenda. The single twenty something son of a millionaire has a different focus than the wife of a disabled veteran. What is important to the farmer in Omaha, Nebraska is not important to the couple in Laguna Beach, California. What is critical to the international family in Brooklyn Heights, NY means absolutely nothing to the small business owner in St. Louis, Missouri. Even within your state and your neighborhood, only you have your agenda. So accepting that we are all individuals with different needs and wants is a start. Accepting this truth can be the start of your freedom.

As you accept the situation you are in you may be angry at first, especially if it is someplace you don't want to be. Once you clearly assess what is going on in your life, once you see the reality then make the best of it. Focus on the reality of your job, home, state, or relationship.

Achieving Fulfillment

Don't tolerate it. Embrace it. First you have to see and acknowledge your heinous living conditions before you can do what you can to make it better.

Ground yourself in the present and learn to love where you are. Obviously, staying in a mentally or physically abusive relationship is not ok, but you first have to ACCEPT that you are in an abusive relationship and then decide that it is not what you want. Only then can you begin to have the strength to gather the resources that you need to leave.

In acceptance there is a freedom that angry stubborn people will never know. Acceptance helps you to get better, do better and know better. Fretting about anything keeps you rooted in the same place as long as you rebel against it. Accepting people places and things lets you enjoy the journey, your journey. You will be surprised how quickly things change when you completely surrender to your reality.

You can only move on once you accept where you are: literally and figuratively.

THIRD LINK

Complaining Is Not For You

UNLINKED:

B esides the scenario in link #1, this situation actually helped me to realize first hand no one wants to be around a complainer.

When I arrived in Los Angeles I worked retail to pay bills. I soon began booking commercial and television spots. Working a day job while pursuing an acting career is nothing new but the busier my acting career became the more I hated my day job. But loved the steady paycheck. Hated the hours I had to put in.
Booking acting work is great but the checks rarely come every week. Sometimes they do. Sometimes they don't.

Working a forty hour week while auditioning can take its toll.

Woman A worked at a job to pay her bills. She was happy to have the work at the beginning, but over time she grew to dislike her job. Immensely. There was no room for advancement and she became miserable. Woman A whined about the job to her friends whenever she made time to get together. She constantly criticized everything pointing out the specifics of why her job was horrible and why everyone should agree with her. She kvetched almost daily. Ok daily. She proclaimed her justification in hating her job to anyone that would listen. She even began protesting the ridiculousness of her job while on the job. Most coworkers were happy to oblige her.

One day woman A went to lunch with her friend woman B. After ordering their food, woman A as usual began expressing her annoyance regarding her employment. Woman B immediately interrupted her. "Why don't you find another job so we can talk about something else? You have been bellyaching about that job for over a year. Frankly, I am sick of hearing about it. Please don't mention that job unless you are telling me you have given your two week notice." Woman A was taken aback. Had she really been complaining about this job for over a year? That day woman A gave her two week notice. This is a true story. I am woman A.

LINK:

No complaining!?! Some of you may close this book right here and never open it again. Don't complain? Really? You may want to complain about being asked to not complain but let's not go there.

 Complaining is fun. Complaining is comfortable. It's so easy to complain. You'd feel like you would be missing out on something if you didn't indulge yourself.

 Complaining is not just expressing your dissatisfaction with a person, place or thing, it is an ongoing tirade about something that affects you on a personal level. Think about your average day. How many times have you not only complained, but pursued a day long diatribe? Constantly complaining is a great way to feel like you are having an effect on the world around you. The longer you complain just maybe your negative words will influence the situation and it will change. We see that it doesn't work that way.

Complaining just makes you unhappy, unapproachable and a whirlwind of negativity. Try to remember the difference between complaining and expressing yourself when something isn't right for you. This can be a tough distinction especially if you are not used to speaking up for yourself.

Complaining usually involves constant griping about something you can not change or are not willing to change.
Constant griping.
Something you can NOT change.
Or NOT WILLING to change.

Expressing yourself comes from a place of living in the present

Achieving Fulfillment

(link one) and being in acceptance (link two). If you are in synchronicity with these two links in the chain to your fulfillment, complaining will probably not be on your agenda. You will express yourself, asking questions about what can and cannot be changed.

Picture someone you know who is a chronic complainer. How do you feel about them? Some use complaining as an attention tool. That is their choice. You might even offer valid solutions to their problems which they quickly thwart. They will tell you that you don't understand how terrible it is for them. Their self pity is full blown. You have the choice to ignore them, or keep your thoughts constructive and stay positive. You don't have to pile on even if you agree with them 100%. Remember, either the situation can not be changed or the individual is not willing to change.

Now, think about what usually happens when you complain. Rarely does anyone say, "I hear you. That's too bad. You must be miserable." Regrettably, a little compassion is what folks are looking for when they first express themselves. When they don't get it, the complain train begins to roll
Usually complaints are met with one up-man-ship. "You think you have it bad? Well, you should see what I have to deal with..." The pity you seek is never available to you. In other words, self pity gets you no sympathy. You think it will, but it never does. Complaining is not for you.

It is possible to get through life without complaining. First you must be aware that you are in fact doing so. Then look at what is bothering you. If you are passionate enough to complain, then you can turn those complaints into productive actions. Always seek solutions. Life is filled with difficulties and complications. Put your problems in two categories; ones you can do something about, and the ones you can not.

The problems you can do nothing about you accept it as reality then let it go. Let it go. Let. It. Go. People lying to you or not returning your phone calls is out of your hands. Remember the first link in your chain to achieving fulfillment? Stay in your truth.
The other category of problems that you can do something about, do it. Complaining about politicians? Read up on the issues and then vote. Your schools are not up to par? Volunteer when you can. One hour a month can make a difference to many. Money in short supply? Do we ever have enough? Be honest with yourself. We can always save a few bucks here and there if we stop complaining that we don't have enough and tune into rearranging our cash flow. How many snacks do we really need? Challenge yourself to problem solve. Challenge yourself to take action to solve your problems so you will eliminate the need to complain. Lip service is easy. Start to question yourself and your choices. Make it a weekly/montgame to see how little you have to complain about.
See how much better you feel after a few months of stepping up and taking action.

The third link to your well being is to take action. Discussing the same idea over and over is not taking action. Like that old expression beating a dead horse, *complaining is a waste of time.* If you find you are asking the same advice from friends and family over and over and not taking it, if you find yourself engaging in a conversation on the same topic of your dismay over and over, then you are complaining, stuck in the problem and not in the solution. If you are unhappy with any part of your life complaining will not change it. Your actions and working these links will help you to move toward feeling better about yourself and your life..

FOURTH LINK

Speak Up When Something Is Wrong

UNLINKED:

S peaking up when something is wrong is basically about having self respect and self preservation. Apparently I was lacking both of these for a long while. I've been in a great many situations where I should have spoken up but I didn't. Trying to find one that was actually humorous was tough, but seek and ye shall find.

I have a very small head. Coconut head and pea head are some of the loving names I was called as a kid. My hair has always been relatively short because for me (and mom growing up) it was easier to care for. In my early thirties I let my hair grow. During that time pursuing my career in NYC, I secured an audition for a soap opera. Still in my do-it-alone phase I thought it would be a great idea to get a fancy new hair-do to impress the casting people who would be auditioning me.

Friends had told me about an upscale hairdresser on the upper East side. Initially I knew that place was way too pricey for a struggling actor, but I was set to book that job so I decided that cost was irrelevant. After all I was going to be working full time.

Once in the beauty parlor my gut told me to leave. I didn't listen. The woman assigned to do my hair was clearly a new nervous wreck. I was undeterred. Nothing wrong here. Keep going. She straightened, washed and started cutting, no chopping at my hair. Finally I spoke up.

> "Uh, this doesn't look like I hoped…"
> "Just wait I'm not finished!"

This made her even more neurotic and she took an even bigger pair of shears to my head.

When she was finished the lump in my throat was so huge I literally could not speak.
Staring back at me in the mirror was a squirrel. Everyone knows what a squirrel looks like. Well that is exactly what I looked like, little ears included.

Still mortified, the next day I awkwardly showed up at my audition. They bring me in to read and put me on camera. I am nervous and embarrassed. During the read I catch a glimpse of myself while I'm auditioning and then is when the lump in my throat dissolves. A small tear forms in my right eye, gains in size and momentum and cascades down my cheek. Obviously they couldn't see how a crying squirrel would capture the hearts and imagination of daytime viewers.

LINK:

Speaking up for yourself is a necessary part of life, whether it be with strangers or loved ones. If we were living in an all loving, all respecting empathetic society this link would still be necessary. Someone can be the sweetest nicest person you know, if they serve you a burger with mushrooms and you absolutely hate mushrooms so you ordered your burger without them and they still served them to you, speaking up is what you do. Unless we all become mind readers, we will always need to be able to speak up for ourselves.

Speaking up is not easy for many. There are those of us who don't like to draw attention to ourselves. Interesting if you think about it. Somewhere in time you have been told or made to feel as if you need to minimize your presence, that you are in the way or that your voice does not matter. Or sometime growing up you were the recipient of too much unwanted attention and you have a tough time letting that go. Since you have hopefully dealt with your past through the work in link one that will be less of an issue for you now. In your aforementioned quest to fly under the radar, opportunities to right a wrong are often not seized. You have a right to speak up. You have a right to be heard. These terms are usually used for demonstrations, protests, rallies, and emailing your congress folk. They also apply to everyday life without the shouting.

Achieving Fulfillment

When you speak up for yourself, it is a reminder that you matter, that you are important. Do not allow others to pick away at who you are. Sometimes when something is wrong it is just an honest mistake. Other times it is someone trying to take advantage of you. It is part of your trek to fulfillment to speak up regardless of what you think is going on.

How you address the situation is important. From receiving the wrong food in a restaurant to incorrect instructions at work to rude and disrespectful people or children; you can address all these situations calmly yet with a varied amount of intensity. Let's go back to the hamburger served with mushrooms. Speaking to your waiter to remedy the food order can be done as casually as if you were ordering something new. You could choose to not take action and complain to your dinner guest throughout the entire meal how much you hate mushrooms and that it's no trouble you can just eat around them. Since complaining is not for you (link three) you take action. No need to grovel, or belittle the waiter, just make your point. The waiter, chef, has the responsibility to correct the mistake. You have no control over them if they decide to be angry. (link two) Your job in life is to be as happy and fulfilled as you can possibly be. Speaking up for yourself helps you to stay that way.

This is more than dining etiquette. When you can speak up regarding the small missteps it becomes easier to voice your concerns when larger issues arise. At your place of employment you might need to flex a bit more muscle.

In a professional setting no matter how casual or formal, speaking up for yourself is an important part of being fulfilled.

Remember, you are speaking up because something is wrong; you are not staging a coup. If you stay grounded in the present (link one), accept the reality whether you like it or not (link two), and no complaining (link three) you are halfway there. Keep asking questions until you get the correct answer you seek. By putting together the first three links before you confront a boss, coworker, client or subordinate, you can focus on righting the wrong; not making someone pay for your heartache. *Achieving fulfillment in life usually refers to eliminating drama.* Drama leads to stress and that is certainly not the direction for you.

You will feel better about yourself speaking up without the drama. It may just be that your perception is off; that does happen. The reason for the problem may not be as sinister as you think. If you stay in your cubicle and grouse about how no one tells you anything, or you never seem to know what's going on, you are sure to have a miserable evening knowing you are not standing up for yourself on the simplest scale.

Small accomplishments help to secure the bigger ones. When it comes to people you know, friends, relatives, children, you may love them but you are allowed to speak up to them too. Are they rude to you? Do they speak to you like you are their servant? NO ONE should be allowed to speak to you in a manner that is condescending and demeaning. (even if you happen to be an employed servant.) Obviously when children are young, that is the time to teach them how to communicate but there is nothing wrong with today. A very wise old lady declared, "It is not always what you say, but how you say it."

Achieving Fulfillment

How do you feel when someone speaks to you like you are a hated inanimate object? Everyone wants to be happy and fulfilled. Some people believe the only way they can feel better about themselves is to make you feel as if you are less than, or don't count. There is no reason to let them use you in this manner.

From kids to coworkers, spouses to strangers do not allow yourself to be belittled. Speak up. You accept people as they are. That is not a reason to accept their bad behavior that directly affects you while you are in their presence. Speak up! When someone is rude, firmly tell them not to speak to you in such a manner and mean it. Stare them dead in the eyes and make your point. It is not about fighting; it is about teaching people how to treat you.

You are grounded, present and accepting. You also speak up when something is wrong or unfair because you matter. Training yourself to speak up adds to your happiness. Opening your mouth when you aren't being treated correctly is part of living a fulfilled life. When you are being talked down to or taken advantage of, you don't feel good.

Short of violence (making any kind of physical contact) do what you can to right your wrong. Don't let issues drag on for days, months or hopefully not, years. Address issues (business or personal) quickly and appropriately. If a customer service issue is at a dead end, ask to speak to their boss. Ask for proof of their claims if you don't believe the information you are receiving. Speaking up involves having clarity. If you can't understand what a salesperson is saying ask them again and again until you understand. Work on the fear of speaking up. It should not outweigh your love for yourself trying to be happy.

Be responsible for yourself. People will try to intimidate you. Or even ignore you if they think they can. Many insecure people, bullies, may even raise their voice or call you names to scare you. Maybe you are scared, but you can still speak up. Stay in the moment. Practice those links, remain calm and restate your needs. Change takes time. Practice speaking up for yourself as much as you can. Keep trying. Never give up on yourself.

Remaining calm and not allowing yourself to become too emotional will help you be in control as you attempt to right a wrong done to you. Most adults secretly feel a bully wins and nice guys finish last. *Be nice but don't finish last.* The person who has borrowed money expects you to be too nice to speak up and ask for repayment. ("Oh, you don't have any cash on you? I will walk with you to the ATM...") An executive who has stolen your brilliant work idea or heavily borrowed from your report and passed it off as theirs expects you to be too nice to speak up and acknowledge the disrespect and injustice. ("Love your work. It is just like the report I wrote last week." Helpful if said in meeting around others. Make sure you keep smiling.) You will have surprise and right on your side when you stand up and speak up for yourself.

Achieving Fulfillment

Your personal relationships are important and also your backbone. Standing up for yourself here may be tougher but it weighs heavily on your ability to be happy and fulfilled in this crazy life. Communicating to those close to you when something isn't right in a timely manner keeps you from becoming a time bomb. You take it, take it, take it, take it and then you explode when you are pushed too far. That is not behavior for a healthy supportive relationship. It is material for some reality show about family members that kill each other. When you explode, this side of violence, you are not teaching people how to treat you. You are lying in wait to ambush them.

Harboring negative feelings over long periods of time is not a link in the chain to achieve fulfillment. Speaking up is on that chain. You deserve love, kindness, understanding and patience. If someone can't give you that, or vice versa, time to rethink your commitment to that person. Always speak up if you aren't getting what you need. You will be happy you did.

FIFTH LINK

Live Fearlessly

UNLINKED:

Not recklessly or lawlessly, but fearlessly. On the surface it appears that I have always lived fearlessly. As we know things are not always what they seem. Hiding my troubles and lack of self-esteem I took a great deal of chances in my life. Living fearlessly is not about making insane choices that you know will haunt you years to come. It is about saying yes to something that (potentially) leads you even further down the path of becoming who you need to be. One of my biggest regrets of not living fearlessly was saying no to entering the Miss Amtrak contest.

Achieving Fulfillment

It was late spring of 1982, the year I took off school to reconcile that studying medicine was not working for me. I took a job at a flooring company since I didn't grow up with the luxury or the choice to spend time 'finding myself'. Since most of my college buddies had all returned to school, I took off Friday and Thursday after work I caught a train to Boston to visit them for the weekend.

Having graduated from bus travel (see link #2) to train travel I looked forward to my journey. And I was dressed for it. My mother always impressed upon me to look presentable in public. Her mother cemented the same don't-look-like-a-slob-pull-it-together mentality in her. As my Uncle Frank would say, "Don't be a crumb". My outfit and attitude was Jackie O meets Diahann Carroll. Classic linen light blue skirt, matching jacket with three quarters sleeve, black with small white polka dot kitten heel pumps, simple lightweight sleeveless tasteful blouse /scarf that matched the heels and a small black purse. My hair was short, but back then it was straightened to within an inch of its life and I was giving a nod to Lola Falana, or trying to, with my curling iron up top and flat back hugging the nape of my neck. Touch of Avon red lipstick and I was ready to make the almost five hour journey from NYC to Boston.

Once onboard I got settled in my seat. Looked out the window, read my book and about two hours in rose to get something to eat. Back to my seat, more window gazing, a little reading and then a bathroom break. Returning from the restroom freshened up, I noticed a number of conductors walked by and acknowledged me. I returned the smiles and greetings and dove back into my book. More conductors walked by doing the same thing. I thought how many of these guys are on this one train and why do they all have to say hi to me?

Donna Cooper

Finally one of them introduced himself and explained that they were looking for someone to enter their beauty contest from the east coast. Of course (of course!) I scoffed just like any other low self esteem scared twenty something would. When they showed me forms and papers and pictures and I realized that this indeed was a real offer I froze. I was deathly afraid. Afraid that I would stand out and own my looks? Afraid that my friends would think I was shallow and stupid for entering a beauty pageant of sorts? It wasn't to be glamourous or televised like the pageants I grew up watching. They wanted someone who looked good, was friendly and had some intelligence to ultimately represent Amtrak.

I remember the feeling of wanting to say yes but I couldn't. The fear of the unknown was more a fear of not trusting myself to deliver. I was already behaving in a way that attracted their attention but I was afraid to say yes because I wasn't comfortable being myself in front of others. To this day I always wonder where my life would have gone had I left that flooring company to pursue Amtrak fame and fortune. Granted I went back to school to ultimately get my degree in drama but I always felt I missed a turn off. I felt as if I chose to not show up in my life. It wasn't about the contest, it was about the people I would have met, the experience of winning. Or losing. Ok, maybe there wasn't any fame or fortune to be had, but I admit the things I've said 'no' to out of fear remind me to live fearlessly today.

LINK:

Words can be easily spoken. It is easy to embrace rhetoric, platitudes, kitschy sayings that are meant to give encouragement to get you through a bad day or a stressful section of your life.

Putting those words into action has always been the challenge. Living fearlessly is an important link in your chain. Let's break down what is meant by living fearlessly. It is easier to tackle an issue (or a cake), piece by piece as opposed to trying to cram the whole thing into you at one time. On this we can all agree.

Using the link system of this book, we acknowledge and accept reality, the second link, which means accepting the presence of fear in our lives. From spiders to heights, small spaces to crazy clowns we have fears. Generally speaking these fears don't really affect us too much on a daily basis thankfully. Living fearlessly speaks to the fears that keep us from living the life that allows us to be fulfilled.

Living fearlessly can evoke images of living a life of adventure. Cliff diving, skydiving, shooting down white water rapids; fun for some but the fear addressed here lies within ourselves. Fear of speaking up (fourth link) can be just the tip of the iceberg. The adult daughter would rather jump from a plane than tell her father to respect her and speak to her in an appropriate manner. Fear of abandonment from the father? The adult son would rather race cars than come to terms with childhood abuse that has made him feel less than. Fear of a life with love and respect? The forty something folk who are so afraid of being hurt or not being accepted for who they are never venture out of their carefully constructed world that perhaps only involves themselves and a safe family member; child or parent?

Donna Cooper

Fear is a condition that can give you the false sense that you are doing the right thing for yourself when actually you are backing yourself into a corner making your world smaller and smaller. Fear makes you think you are protecting yourself when in fact you are cutting yourself off. To live without fear is to work these links, and know you want the best possible life for yourself.

Achieving Fulfillment

Originally this link was called 'Give Up The Paranoia'. The word paranoia sounded a bit too precious (like calling your notebook a journal; see the first link). What is appropriate about the word paranoia is that it does help to highlight the focus of this link.

Living fearlessly really means to live a life unencumbered by your past and in acceptance of the future.

Living fearlessly means having courage (having fear but taking the action anyway).

Doing more in your life to show yourself that you will not die if you approach a stranger to ask them out. You will gain more from doing rather than choosing to stay cloaked in your fear blanket. Calling it paranoia speaks to the cunning way it infiltrates life.

Definition of paranoia:
A form of chronic insanity usually characterized by persecution, fears, suspicion and well organized imaginary thoughts.

Ever hear someone discuss a hot button issue, say gun control, and really listen to what they are saying? Many folks that have a small arsenal of automatic weapons, etc, etc truly believe that someone is going to make them give up their weapons and that the government is coming to take over their property. Regardless of political party no one has mentioned anything to give this thought validity. Now reread the definition for paranoia. Unless you are diagnosed by a psychiatrist that you indeed clinically have this mental illness, you can help yourself. This particular issue is a good example because anyone can do the research, look at the facts and see that the fear these people experience is unfounded. It is based on their own made up ideas.

This is not about guns. It is about examining your fears. Finding out where they come from and why you keep them alive. This is about you looking at what really scares you. Dive into what keeps you from making a new friend, asking someone out for coffee, or taking a well deserved vacation. This is about the first four links of this book and you achieving well deserved peace in your life. Whatever you have gone through, you deserve to be happy. Yes, that is why this book is all about you.

Apparently people are scary. When was the last time someone held the door for you and you looked them in the eyes, smiled and said thank you? When was the last time you held the door for some else and then said have a nice day? When have you called someone who may not be a close friend but you know they are struggling in one way or another and asked how they were? When was the last time you looked your spouse in the eyes and said, "I love you"? Many times we wait for others to make the first move. That is the safe thing to do. What are you really afraid of? Getting your feeling hurt? OK fair enough. So does that mean you will never extend your hand and introduce yourself to someone new on the job, or new in the neighborhood, or at a holiday party?

No one wants their feelings hurt, but focusing on the hurt keeps you shut down and in the past. You might have been hurt but realize you are alive and you lived through it. Not every encounter will result in bruised feelings. Why keep those negative thoughts and experiences alive by acting on them constantly? You have the ability to reduce the fear in your heart with small steps. As they say what doesn't kill you makes you stronger. What doesn't kill you CAN make you stronger if you choose to empower yourself.

Make sure the information you have running around in your head is at least based on fact. It is easy to get the negative story from media because fear is what gets you to stay up late and watch the nightly news. Many in the name of journalism say outrageous things that get people to listen because that is their job to garner high ratings and keep you watching. You have a brain, a mind of your own. Just because someone tells you something on the radio or television does not make it true.

Most people have a general fear of the unknown. Why not try having a curiosity about the unknown? Don't get your information all from one place. Develop your common sense.
Being fearful means you are easily manipulated. Who wants to be manipulated? NO ONE. So stop.
Stop listening to the negativity, or at least listen with ½ an ear. Being fearful may keep you out of a back alley at three in the morning, but fears will also make you hate people, follow the wrong crowd, live in a box and generally be miserable.

Yes, bad things can happen to good people. Bad things happen to all people at some time or another. You don't need to look for them or expect them to happen to you. If you feel like bad things always happen to you then they will. Check your facts, bad things happen to all of us. Do only bad things happen to you? If your past has been riddled with heinousness you will have to work harder at being less afraid. You will have to strive daily to put together positive experiences.

You are allowed to change the way you think. You are allowed to be present and lessen the chances of bad things happening to you.

Everyone has read those horrible emails about someone waiting to slit your throat at the mall, or steal your identity. Basically the news tells us they are out to get you.

Even if everyone is honestly out to get you, you are not a sitting duck. You are engaged in your life, staying in the moment and thinking positively. You reject the fear. You are stronger than that. If you do not feel like you are right now, just act like you are. It really is just practice. You are building up your positive muscles. It takes time. Work one link at a time and you won't even have to think about being positive or unafraid. You will just be.

Your worst fears will probably never come true so stop calling them into your consciousness. You truly do get what you ask for. How many times out of frustration have you said I just want to be left alone? You repeat that over and over you are readying yourself to be by yourself. You do get what you ask for. Look at the people you consider lucky. Listen to them. Bet you never hear them say, "nothing good ever happens to me." Even if they have experienced some setbacks they still get up and expect good things. They don't live in fear.

Being fearful in life is not just about staying inside and never exploring the world around you. Fear can have a very unhealthy effect on you and how you deal with relationships. An example is what some call the hostage syndrome. Have you ever been taken hostage? This is where the person you are with is really jealous and prefers you not to go anywhere besides work without them? Or they do not want you to really have any friends of your own? Everything has to be filtered through them to get their seal of approval. If you are in a relationship and you feel as if any of the above mentioned themes are prevalent, address it immediately. If you are the one being the 'hostage taker' know that hostages just want to get away. (and eventually they do.)

At first it may seem as if the 'hostage taker' cares about you completely. As you can see from the outside, what is really going on is that the 'hostage taker' is extremely insecure. There is a lack of self love. Or perhaps some emotional trauma in their past that they have not dealt with or truly recovered from. The 'hostage taker' can be afraid of a number of things. This book isn't about a medical diagnosis. It is about recognizing the changes you need to make in your life to achieve fulfillment. If you are someone who grabs onto another and expects them to fulfill your every need, please do some work on freeing yourself and your 'hostages' from this debilitating practice.

Try working these links. No one of us gets through life unscathed. The tragedy is when you know your behavior is basically hurtful, but your fears keep you from changing. No one wants to hurt themselves or anyone else if they claim to love them.

Achieving Fulfillment

Paranoia in society can keep you from seeing the world, helping others, and fulfilling dreams. You can find dozens of frightening reasons why you should never leave your hometown. Again, common sense will tell you some choices are better than others for places to vacation, but still go.

You may want to move to another state or country, but don't because of the crime rate or sex offenders in that state or it is just easier to stay put. Try looking at the upside of the move. Try trusting that you have good ideas and if something is nagging at you to move, go! ***Check out the positive and know you can handle the negative. Don't let fear keep you down.*** Stay in the now and refuse to be a scaredy-cat. Act as if until you really believe it.

Face your fear, paranoia and see if it makes sense. Yes, unfortunately we see plane crashes but hundreds of planes take off and land safely everyday. Focus on that. Yes, unfortunately people get cancer, but if you stop smoking, eat more fruits and vegetables and get some regular exercise you lessen your cancer chances (as well as other illnesses, heart disease etc) dramatically. Yes unfortunately, some people get robbed, so don't talk so much about how much money you have, carry limited cash and pay attention. Focus on the present and positive solutions.

Fear will steal away your potential, your interesting dreams and your life enriching experiences. Your paranoia will keep you hostile, alone and feeling like a victim. These links along with some trust can change your fearful way of thinking. Stop believing everything you hear. Don't be lazy; get the facts. Say aloud what scares you most or write it down then smile and run down why that will not happen to you.

Donna Cooper

Do not let fear take away your ability to achieve fulfillment.

SIXTH LINK

Take Care Of Basics

UNLINKED:

When I first moved to LA my goal was to work as actress. What I didn't take into account was that I needed to take care of myself first. I struggled to acclimate to the weather, 345 days of sunshine, 15 days of torrential rain, bad attitudes, and ghastly traffic. On top of that I was trying to find a place to live and make money to survive. I impulsively moved with a very small amount of money ($50) and slept on a friend's couch while trying to 'make it big'.

I'm not necessarily criticising my choices. I'm highlighting the fact that I did not make room in my grand plan for myself. I didn't focus on the basics of life which often left me cranky and depressed. I was more than miserable often in those early days because I would spend money on a new outfit and not have any cash for 3 square meals. Sometimes one meal was all I'd manage.

I would buy the most expensive cosmetics trying to think like a 'star'.

Talking to a girlfriend on the phone one day I was particularly miserable. I had started going to Alcoholics Anonymous. I hadn't been drinking lots but I was so miserable and I *wanted* to drink loads so I went to the meetings. They espouse the use of the the acronym HALT. Do not allow yourself to be hungry, angry, lonely or tired. My friend who was not in the program said she was worried about me as I continued sobbing in her ear.

"Have you eaten anything today?", she asked quietly, "maybe eat something and then take a nap?"

I exploded.

"How do you know about HALT?!? How do you know about eating and resting! You're not in program!!"

I wish I could have had this book to remind me of the the basics. Sometimes we forget.

LINK:

If you choose to work this sixth link suggesting you take care of basics, you will have the foundation for a physically happier you. Taking care of the basics is taking care of the obvious which is often ignored. Your goal is to be as happy and fulfilled as you can be. Links one through five have you on your way. You have one body and one mind; that is as basic as you can get. Let's focus on how we need to take care of them.

At first glance, these basics are obvious. You might do these ten sub links for a month, feel better, then go back to some of your old less productive habits.

Achieving Fulfillment

Try to get to a place where these sublinks become second nature and you will be sharing these simple ideas with those around you who will be enjoying a happier you.

Sublink #1
Eat breakfast everyday.

Very simple. It doesn't have to be Eggs Benedict or bagels, cream cheese, capers and smoked salmon and pitchers of mimosas everyday. (Though that does sound lovely). It doesn't even have to be something thought of as a breakfast food. Eat the other half of your leftover sandwich from lunch yesterday. It could be a bottled smoothie juice drink, or some peanut butter on some crackers. Or a banana...or a piece of cold pizza just eat something to break the fast. This is not about dieting or not dieting. It is about common sense. You have gone at least six hours(and that is perhaps a minimum) without any food. Our bodies need to eat to survive and keep us functioning properly. When we starve ourselves our bodies don't feel as good. Those of you that don't eat some kind of breakfast are challenging your body to survive unnecessary self inflicted abuse. Neglecting to eat anything until lunch (or even dinner) stresses the body. It will eventually cave from the abuse. You are inviting ulcers, colon problems the list goes on and on. Not to mention you know how well you do or don't function when you're hungry. Decision making is probably not up to snuff. This sublink is not about creating fear; it's about accepting the facts about the way the body works. Ask someone with digestive tract or organ issues. With the links you have found a better way to live your life. Continue to help yourself. Eat SOMETHING for breakfast everyday.

Sublink #2.
See A Doctor Once A Year

Again, obvious but please do it regardless of the cost. It is your responsibility as an adult to have health insurance. If you don't you are living like a child burying your head in the sand pretending that your body will last forever. Remember this book is all about taking care of yourself, and reaching goals you have set for yourself. A fortunate by product of using these links is that those that depend on you and love you will be happy you are loving yourself. You already know the car analogies. Stop pretending that your body is someone else's problem. Don't burden your family, friends (and finances) only going to see a doctor when it is a dire emergency because by then it most certainly will be. Get a full check up. Your Ob-Gyn does not count as a full check up! But you knew that already.

Sublink #3.
See A Dentist

The dentist gets put on the back burner usually for financial reasons. Oh, and that drilling sound and perhaps the pain that might be involved. If you are going to neglect this doctor until you have excruciating mouth/tooth pain at least be proactive. Put it in your budget to purchase mouthwash and floss when you buy toothpaste. Flossing daily, even once a day, and using one of the many varieties of mouthwashes available to you and brushing after breakfast, lunch and dinner (because you eat breakfast now) can keep cavities and pain and the dentist at bay. But you should still go once a year. You clean the pots and pans and plates to get rid of food particles.

Your mouth deserves the same thorough treatment as a roasting pan. The health of your mouth is part of keeping your body healthy. Try not to see taking care of yourself as a burden or annoying. The ability to take care of yourself reflects how much you value yourself and you should. The more you care for yourself while you are able, it lessens the possibility that someone will have to take care of you as you age. No guarantees but why not give it your best shot?

Sublink #4
Do Something Each Day That Can Be Called Exercise

Relax. This is not about spending lots of cash on a gym membership or buying expensive equipment. This is about approximately 20 minutes of getting in touch with your muscles, whatever state they are in.

When you get out of bed in the morning stretch your arms up to try to touch the ceiling and then hang down and try to touch your toes. Take a few deep breaths in with your yawns. This can take ten seconds or ten minutes depending on how much time you have.

Do the same thing before you sit down at your desk. Who cares what a co-worker may think? You are doing what you need to do to take care of yourself. Always take the stairs instead of the elevator if you have the choice. Find ways during the day to remind your body that you remember it is the only one you have. Stretch while you are watching your morning talk shows.

Do it right before you have lunch. Do it after lunch. Do it before you get in the car to drive home. Do it before you clean up the kitchen at night. Do it before and after you brush your teeth. Do it.

Hopefully you already have an exercise regime in place. If not, keep looking for ways to get some and start with the morning stretch. This is the ONLY body you have. Love it enough to keep it healthy. You don't have to have abs of steel but you need a steel resolve to stay healthy.

Sublink #5.
Eat More Fruits And Vegetables And Drink More Water

Do not obsess over this one. See this as routine as showering everyday. Accept (second link) and don't complain (third link) that your body functions better and longer if you eat vegetables and fruit and drink lots of water. No one is taking away your soda, or cheez-its or chocolate yummies. Each day think about (then do it) how you can add more of these three things to your daily food intake. When someone mentions giving up chips, or your go to snack foods we panic and say never. By incorporating the links into your life you are looking for a better healthier way. Add in the fruits, veggies and more water and automatically your snack craving should decrease. Again this is not a book on dieting or how to lose weight. Your body will feel better and even perhaps look better with more water in your system. Your body is made up of water not soda so help it out. Make a point to carry out this sublink day in and day out and feel better about yourself. It is all about you.

Sublink #6.
Eliminate A Vice

We all have them, big or small. Try eliminating one major one even if you have tried before. Keep trying until you quit. Never stop trying even if you keep failing.

Don't stay down. That cigarette may be laced with all kinds of addictive things in addition to the nicotine, so you have to try even harder to stop. Use every product you can get your hands on to release the vice. Be responsible for your actions. Get outside help if you need it. Reading the links and doing what you can to clean house and be happy is not always an easy road. Vices usually make us feel better for the moment. When your life is made up of a series of things we do for immediate gratification there is usually long term health issues to deal with in the future. This is not crazy paranoia. These are facts that you have chosen to ignore.

Don't traumatize your family by dying before your time (which is hopefully somewhere near 101 or 2) Don't burden your family and country financially to pay to keep you alive when you are actively not caring enough about yourself to quit. You know your vice(s). It could be smoking, drinking too much, over medicating with prescription drugs, overeating/bingeing, or anything else you know you do that is truly harmful and unsafe for your body and mind. Get rid of at least one and who knows? The others may follow.

Sublink #7.
Get A New Bed

You are focused on the body. Now you can also nurture the mind. This is essential. Your bed is the one place you go everyday for comfort and peace. Do not compromise on a good bed for yourself. Never buy or sleep in a used bed (hotels and the occasional futon at a friends are exceptions). Get a new mattress (and box spring) at least every ten years. If you can afford to do it sooner great. Your bed is the one constant that lets you get a good night sleep. You are going to sleep anyway.

Why not make it really work for you? You need it to survive. And thrive. If you say you can't afford a new one, ask for a mattress set for your birthday or as a holiday gift. Or at least gift certificates or money toward it. Having a good bed to sleep in allows your body and mind to harmonize at night so you can be present in your life each day. Think about how you feel when you haven't slept well. Put a new mattress on the top of your list as one of the basic necessities you need for a happier you.

Watch for sales on mattress sets. Forget the expensive frame for now and get a decent mattress. They will deliver, take away and set up. There is no excuse for not having the one main instrument required for recharging yourself. You have what you need to recharge your cell phone. When it rains you put on a raincoat and take an umbrella. You don't put on a wool sweater and carry a golf club (unless you are my husband). Get the right tool for the job. The job is restoring you to some semblance of sanity every night and preparing you to wake ready to have a great day. Go test a few. Then buy one. (There are no stores or mattress manufacturers goading me or giving me money to say this. It is just another fact.)

Sublink #8.
Do Something Nice For Someone

Since you are doing such a good job of loving yourself and taking good care of yourself it is time to spread the love. Hopefully you are already kind to your immediate family. It is time to get out of your comfort zone. Do something for someone outside of your immediate family bubble. You will be surprised how great you will feel when you make someone's day. Call or visit a senior citizen, relative or not, that is home all day alone. Give five dollars to the kid selling candy bars for his school. Help someone load groceries in their car and don't take any money for it. There are a lot of people in this world that are lonely, infirmed and would love to have someone smile at them and recognize that they matter. Perhaps that is how you feel. Even more of a reason to do what you can to connect to someone outside of your daily circle.

Yes, everyone is busy with kids, work, spouse's, home maintenance, the lot. Think for a moment. If you record (or maybe even skip!) one of your shows you have 30 minutes or an hour to make someone's day. Since you are in a positive space you have the time to be thankful for all you have and share your great attitude with others.

Love is not finite. There is plenty to go around. The better you treat yourself the more love you have to share. Spread it around and watch it multiply. Surprise your in-laws with a card just saying hey. Do things for others without expectations of something in return. Try it once a month. Then once a week. Do I dare challenge you to spread love every day?

Sublink #9
Laugh At Yourself

Embrace that you are human with all of the imperfections and laugh at yourself. Embrace your own humanity. Don't mock, jeer or ridicule yourself. Have an honest chuckle at some of the things you do. It will keep you from being so serious. It will keep you from being so hard on yourself. We all make mistakes. We have all done embarrassing things in public or private. So what? If this is new for you, give yourself time to practice. Not one of us is perfect.

Take the time to laugh. At anything. There are always lots of reasons to feel bad, be negative or bitter. Watch the news, read the nonsense online, or just be jealous of those who have more than you. There is always something to help you to be depressed. So try taking a break from the news (you can catch up on the weekend), remember those who are less fortunate than you (there is always someone), work your links and be thankful! Which brings us to sublink ten.

Sublink #10
Be Thankful

Being thankful each day helps to keep your head in the right space. Everyday you can find someone who is not nearly as lucky as you are. When things were not going well in my life, being thankful for the ability to have my motor skills intact and ask for help allowed me to get from one day to the next. So many people in our country, in this world are fighting situations we can only pretend to have a clue what their lives are like. You didn't decide who your parents would be, what socio-economic level they would be, their race, or religion. It was all by chance. You could just as easily have been born halfway around the world to different people.

So be thankful that where you are in life that you have things others don't. Even if it is the ability to vote. Or read. Or marry who you love. Or laugh out loud in public. Get out of the self pity and shine like you are meant to shine. Treat each day like another chance to not only fulfill your destiny, but to help others be the best and happiest they can be.

SEVENTH LINK

Control Yourself

UNLINKED:

Instead of heading to New Orleans during Mardi Gras (usually every March), my group of friends elected to hit Bourbon St and the environs whenever we could to ring in the New Year.

One year I began the journey in Atlanta. Two of us and her boyfriend. Drove to Mississippi to pick up the boyfriend's friend. At this point we added a second car since the friend wanted the option of leaving early.

The plan was to road trip to the New Orleans airport, pick up two more friends, head down to the French Quarter where we had reserved a B&B for the six of us then go party like it was 1999. Actually is was 1999. No it was 1989. Same thing.

Since I had not learned the link of controlling myself, I agreed to ride with my friend's boyfriend's friend. (I was there and it already sounds dodgy.) He convinced me to ride with him by confiding in me we would be making Tanqueray and tonics on the drive down. I'm in.

Needless to say the ride down was a blast. He was funny and cute and the drinks flowed. About time we met up at the airport we were both bombed. Six of us all accounted for, the two we picked up at the airport drove in the other car and I climbed back in the bar car.

We were supposed to meet up at the B&B.

The problem was neither I nor my driver knew the location of the place. He thought I knew and I thought he knew. When you don't control yourself you always figure someone else will be responsible.

Remember, this was before cell phones, we drove around in a haze trying to guess at the location. That didn't work. Finally, we did the only thing people with no self control do. We parked the car and hit Bourbon St. We had a ball drinking even more, dancing, laughing and making new friends.

We spent the night carousing since we had no clue how to find our friends. We slept a couple of hours in the car. I wasn't sad at all.

Next day we headed back to one of our favorite bars hoping to run into our buddies. Nothing. This guy and I ate, drank and hit the scene as if we had just awoken from a great night's rest.

Night began to fall again on the Quarter. We chose a bar to ring in the new year with lingering thoughts of our friends and that elusive B&B.

Thirty minutes before midnight our friends walked in the door. Yes we celebrated like long lost comrades being reunited, because we were. Soon our friends, who were angst ridden because of our disappearance grew tired and wanted to leave. My lost friend and I weren't ready to leave. Our friends grew impatient with our revelry and left. Once again each one of us thought the other had gotten the directions or at the least the address of the place we were supposed to be staying. Neither of us did. Another night out roaming the the streets. Upsetting good friends, ignoring my own safety, 48 hours of straight drinking lead to alcohol poisoning and finally swearing off jello shots (remember those?). Ok it was the second to last time I did jello shots. The last time involved throwing up in a pile of a strangers clean laundry but enough proof that the seventh link is a necessary one to lead a healthy happy life.

LINK:

Controlling yourself starts with controlling your thoughts. Wrestling with the mind can be tough, but you can control your thinking. **That is where your power lies. What goes on in your mind is within your control.** Ideas, memories, anecdotes, pop tunes, wants and needs for the day, week, year randomly pop into your consciousness. It is your choice if you want to dwell on them. Thoughts direct how you feel moment to moment. When your thoughts are worrisome, dark and self pitying, so are you.

When you open your eyes first thing in the morning (or afternoon) and you immediately remember your outstanding debt, your sick relative, the botched kitchen remodel, the unresolved argument with your sibling, or any other litany of negative occurrences personal or public, you are laying the groundwork for a miserable day. Do you want to have a miserable day of fretting? Do you want to be angry and snap when your kids ask if they can go to a friends house? If they ask at all? Do you want to be the negative one in the break room that ALWAYS feels like nothing goes right in your life and you are the one to 'trump' everyone else's tales of woe? You don't want any of this. Let's start over.

You open your eyes and start to remember all the negative. Then you say "wait" or "no". You can even say it out loud. Tell yourself "not now", "don't go there" and actively bring different thoughts into your head. You stand up and stretch. You remember something positive about today, the sixth link, taking care of basics; the good breakfast you will have (sublink #1), some form of exercise today (sublink#4), figuring out which senior citizen to call today to see how they are faring (sublink#9), deciding how much to incorporate sublink#5 into your daily menu, the positive list is just beginning.

You will not forget your woes by pushing them aside for the moment.
So why not give yourself a break? Ruminating on them will not solve them immediately. Thinking and agonizing and worrying and brooding and worrying and stewing and overthinking and worrying does nothing to solve your problems. This behavior turns your stomach sour and over taxes your nervous system. *You are not being cavalier or irresponsible about your obligations by not thinking about them 24/7.*

You are choosing to control yourself. There is a time and place for everything.

When you decide to push aside the anxiety in your head, you are making an active choice to control your thoughts. If you are known to be one who worries, it will take more that one gentle reprimand to stop the incessant obsessing. Accept (second link) that is who you are and work on changing. After two days of guiding your thoughts you still nestle back into the crevice of torment. Keep trying. Sure the goal is to go from worrying 100% of the time to 0%. Even if you get to only 50%, that is progress. Even 85% will give your body a nice respite. Your body is thankful to you for releasing some of its stress. Continue to push aside the ruminations. Continue to guide your thoughts to your present action. Focus on what is right in front of you be it a child, friend, work or television. Focus on what is going on around you not checking your phone every thirty seconds obsessively texting your issues. You are more likely to be inspired with solutions to problems if you are not wringing your hands over them every second of every minute of every day.

If it is still difficult for you to control your thoughts and think positively, go deeper. You wake up in the morning and remember how much you hate your home and you don't have the money to move. You can be a miserable bugger all day feeling sorry for yourself or you can go back to the reality that matters. For now, do you have a roof over your head when it rains and a bed to sleep in? Food to eat? Is there one person in this world that really loves you? If there is one, there are probably two. Being thankful is a great way to stop panicking. (sublink #10).

Control your need to go negative. It is just as easy to think about situations working out in your favor than it is to think that they won't. Interrupt your condition of worrying and negativity. Control yourself.

Controlling yourself is about bringing balance back into your life. Too much of anything is no good like too much worrying. You know the obvious ones like too much drinking or gambling, but too much television, video play, food, work or alone time is not good either. On the flip side no alone time is as crazy making as too much. Too much of one thing, or select things keeps you off balance and out of sync with the life you are meant to lead. Only you know what is the right balance. No one can impose that on you. Work on your balance. Controlling yourself you will be surprised how much better you will feel over time.

It is wise to also control your words. Your thoughts are your own but your words tell the world what you are about, who you are. As you learn to control your thoughts, your words will automatically take on a more positive spin. Run through a few of the things you said yesterday. Were they uplifting and positive, or were they hurtful, arrogant barbs? Perhaps that is an exaggeration, but if your words tend toward the sarcastic that could signify that you are angry and hurt from some past experiences. Reread the first link as many times as you need. Remember balance here. I happen to be a fan of sarcasm until I realised everything out of my mouth was an eye rolling poison dart. I was deeply angry for years and sarcasm was my shield. Sarcasm has its place just not ALL the time. Joking and making light of situations helps you to stay positive. Remember sublink #9.

Again too much of anything is no good. If you are sarcastic all the time, take time to check yourself and figure out what ails you emotionally. Strive for balance.

Controlling your anger is an obvious one. Whether it is yelling and screaming or throwing things and having a full on tantrum, it would be in your best interest to immediately work on how to end this behavior. (Unless you are a gifted two year old reading this and then your parents need to deal with you.). When you're screaming and yelling, NO ONE hears you. They might be standing right in front of you but if you are screaming at them they really just want you to shut up and go away. You are not communicating anything beside your lack of self control. A stern serious tone, even threatening is much more effective with people especially children. If your goal is to be heard, do it in a way that people can hear you. Practice this. It works.

Your life is your business; don't concern yourself with what others may think. Get help and help yourself as you need it. Work these links and sublinks. Learning to control yourself doesn't mean you can never let go or have fun. If you have learned to exercise self control in all areas of your life, you will have a better life experience; from quiet time in the tub to surprise birthday bashes in full swing.

EIGHTH LINK

Stop Doing What Is Not Working

UNLINKED:

When I first decided to pursue a career as a stand-up comic I was coming from a background in acting. My B.A. was in drama and I had taken an array of classes and seminars in NYC after graduation. Jumping into stand-up comedy, I felt confident about being funny but I lacked any kind of chutzpah when it came to networking. The word 'schmooze' haunted me as I watched others book spots at clubs because their friend 'brought them up' (on stage) for a quick 5 or 10 minute set. I reckoned with the word tenacity. Heard it often that along with 'schmoozing' one had to be tenacious. At least perhaps I could do that.

The movie, "Punchline" came out in 1989. Months, or a year or so before that, the scuttlebutt was casting folk were looking to use real stand up comics in the movie. In fact they did. I was not one of them, but not from the lack of trying. I was trying the wrong thing.

Alexa Fogel was the casting director on the movie. I did have a chance meeting with her but so did tons of other comics. In retrospect, she was professional and really nice. She said something like , "keep in touch" or "let me know how things go for you." Well, I took those words as my ticket to fame and fortune. Looked up her number at the casting office and called her almost everyday. For a year. We never spoke. They would put me on hold until after an hour or so I would have to hang up. No cell phones then. Thankfully. I probably would have called her for two years straight. To this day I am thankful she didn't get gag order against me. She is still a brilliant casting director. Alexa Fogel I am so sorry I was so immature and stubborn and misguided that I called your office so often. The fact that I continued to call for so long for no good reason is unforgivable. Wish I'd read this book sooner.

LINK:

Stop doing what is not working. It sounds simple because it is. Putting it into practice is the challenging part. Familiar routine, laziness, lack of imagination are some of the reasons you keep doing the things that you know need to be changed. Habits form over time. Sometimes these habits have become markers of insanity; which you know is doing the same thing over and over expecting a different result. (like the example above) Most of you continue the habit and complain. Since we have eliminated that in the second link, it is time to work on the habit. Change is tough, but not impossible.

It is prudent to identify what exactly is not working in your life. Take some time to sit quietly and go over it in your head or preferably write it down. Know what it is you want out of life. What are your goals? Be specific. If it is to be happy what is it that would make you happy?

You can write down short term goals but make sure you focus on long term goals here. You want to identify what you are doing that keeps you from achieving a life that fulfills you.

Focus on what it is you are doing day in and day out. Which activities are leading you into a dead end? Which daily habits are keeping you from reaching your goals?

Are you trying to quit smoking but you make a point to take your morning break with the other smokers? Trying to move ahead at the job but you are chronically late for work? Trying to get in better shape and your lack of water and sweet tooth hold you back? Trying to put a spark back in your relationship and your around-the-house outfits don't reflect confidence or a willing sexuality? Trying to save money and budget and you are constantly leaving change and bills in your pockets to be washed into shreds? Trying to have a better social life yet you never call or initiate any kind of get together or ask anyone out on a date?

After identifying what isn't working, then take one at a time. Say you are tackling your inability to woo your spouse because you are always too tired. Try forgoing your television routine for one night and go to bed early. The folks on television or Netflix or YouTube most certainly will not miss you.

Once you have figured out what you do that does not move you in the direction of happiness and fulfillment, altering your actions can be easier than expected. It can also initially make you a little cranky.

Donna Cooper

As you make changes you are getting out of your comfort zone. There will be a certain amount of resistance, inner kicking and crying that will happen. You get used to eating ½ a bag of chips every night while catching up on your recorded evening dramas. You decide to change. The kid in you is mad.

Achieving Fulfillment

The savvy adult that you are becoming knows it is for the best. Whether it be getting to bed earlier to have some fun with your significant other (or so you can get to work on time) or simply swapping the chips for carrot sticks you know these changes are necessary to move you in a direction that makes you feel better about your life.

Keep your goals in sight to help pull you through the uncomfortable feelings. Go easy on your yourself. It took awhile for you to develop some of these habits. Give yourself time to make the shift. Allow time for new habits to be ingrained. It can take time. You are free to continue to do what isn't working but why would you want to stay in that place?

Make a plan for yourself. It may take a week, month, or even just a day to adopt new habits. It might take a year. Try not to move on to another issue to be changed until you have actually altered the initial pattern. This is your life. You want things to happen quickly, but be patient. Start altering your routine today and by next year, or for some next month, you will have stopped ineffectual behavior and be a lot happier with your life.

NINTH LINK

Believe In Something Greater Than Yourself

UNLINKED:

Trying to make a living in show business for me also involved having to make a living while trying to make a living. Since the age of fourteen I worked not only to have lunch money but to contribute financially to my family when I could. So going after my dreams meant stepping on the gas pedal even harder.

It was all about me. I worked a day job and odd jobs to pay my bills. I saved (sometimes!) for any splurges I wanted. I depended on myself to get myself better when sick, to keep decent clothes on my back and to fight any battles that came my way. I.I.I. Me.Me.Me. I was wonder woman until I got tired.

I can remember doing a stand up gig out of town and I mailed my rent check from there. It didn't make it to my landlord on time.

The list of things that went wrong from there would take another 100 pages to divulge. At this time I didn't practice any particular religion. I heard speak of this 'god' being my creator but I didn't have time for anything that wasn't right in front of me moving me forward in life. When my world started to crumble emotionally and financially, no one in my circle helped. Mostly because I didn't ask for any. I took care of myself. I went to the beach...NOT a summer day. I cried and cried and felt all the delicious self pity I could muster. Then I had an epiphany. The ocean. Who worked really hard to get that built? Night was falling. Those stars? Who sweat and toiled to get them up and shining? Something I didn't understand.

Life was hard. (life is hard). Believing that if you work hard and are nice to people everything will be grand. Not true. I didn't understand why I couldn't do it all by myself. After too many tears I was exhausted. Even if my friends had taken up a collection, paid off my bills and treated me like a five year old, I still needed to reconcile that hollow feeling inside that I had daily. Why did seeing the ocean, sunsets, or walks in the woods seem to make me feel better even when my physical world appeared to be crashing down on me?

And that voice. That small voice voice inside of me that always knows the right answer? Isn't that just me being brilliant?

I was like a baby crying and someone plays peek-a-boo. I'd cry and be in self pity. Then I'd think about something greater than myself that can make the world turn and I'd feel better. Then I'd say that's stupid the universe doesn't care about me and I'd cry even harder. The cycle continued for way too long.

LINK:

This is not the religion section. If some of you are actively connected to an organized or unorganized religion, I hope you take what you want from this and you use it to love yourself and others.

If you aren't connected, it is time to get connected. Not to a religion, but to some metaphysical facts that are essential to your happiness.

What comes to mind when you think of something greater than yourself? Do you you believe that anything is more than or greater than you?

The universe is pretty vast and amazing. Comparing yourself to it makes you feel small. You can call the something greater than yourself the universe because it is. Do you remember the name of the woman who started that 'Big Bang' (NOT the television show) with her test tubes of gases and created the stars? What is the name of that guy who formed the atoms that made the oceans? There are many a natural phenomenon that remind us that we are just a tiny piece of the puzzle. A sunset, sunrise, tsunami's, the Grand Canyon; have you figured out the name of the human being who orchestrated all these? Simply put, there is some force of energy that is greater than you. Accepting this fact will help you navigate the insanity of your own world.

Belief is necessary for a calm and balanced life. Even if you don't believe a word of this, try connecting with the energy greater than yourself. Go ahead. No one is watching.

In the quiet time you give yourself, morning, afternoon or evening without television, cell phones, kids, girlfriends or laptops, think about the last full moon you saw, or waterfall or sunset or snow peaked mountain and feel your body relax. Sit quietly. You will find yourself smiling when you recreate that scene of the sun's rays bouncing off topaz blue water. Scenes of the power of the universe can quench like a cool glass of lemonade on a humid day. Please don't knock something until you have tried it a few times. You will be surprised.

Some call something greater than yourself God. Some say god or gods. Some say it is those that have died before us; their energy is still around for us to tap into for guidance. Some call it a higher power. Even if conjuring images of something greater than yourself you believe to just be a load of hooey, believing in SOMETHING helps you to continue on in life without taking your life with its ups and downs so seriously. The comfort (imaginary or real) that you can experience when you know you are invisibly supported by something you can always turn to, it can keep your head out of the oven when life gets really crazy.

When you call a friend to talk and they don't have time for you, when you have given your all to a project and the boss' nephew decides he doesn't like you or your ideas, when children are mistreated and go hungry, when you try so hard to lose weight and you discover you have a life threatening illness, when death comes too soon for a vivacious loved one; when you are emotionally at the end of your logical rope that is exactly when a higher power can get you through ,minute by minute.

No matter how crazy it may sound the energy of the universe is always available to you. No one has all the answers. We just want to be happy.

If the power of the universe, God, god, Karma, those who have gone before, can calm your mind why not open yourself up to it?

Hopefully your life isn't fueled solely by your own selfish desires. Your friendships suffer because it is always about you. As a business partner, you keep your goals in sight and sacrifice anything and anyone, including your business partner to get what you want. If you live in a vacuum, a life driven by selfishness works just fine. Believing in something greater than yourself gives you the freedom to fervently pursue your goals while being mindful of balance in your life. You can be a successful stockbroker without ripping off your mother and her friends. Or maybe ripping off your family is the right thing for you. Only you and the universe know what helps you sleep at night. The slight whisper you hear once in a while is that energy reminding you of what you need to do to stay on track in your life. Some call it a conscience. Some have never heard of the word.

When was the last time you had a peaceful day with people in it? It is easy to be at peace if you lock yourself away and never interact with anyone. It is possible to walk through life with all its realities and misgivings and angst and have a great sense of peace. That peace is part of what will bring you the fulfillment you crave. **Know that you have love, acceptance and a guiding energy ALWAYS available to you. The energy of the universe is with you at all times because you are part of something bigger than yourself.**

God, the universe, a higher power...SOMETHING was out there making the world turn. Science. If the energy is out there to spin this planet there has got to be something to hook into to help me along my journey.

Just the thought of something greater than myself gives me the wherewithal to hang in another day.

Stay connected daily to that entity or energy. You will find wisdom and acceptance, hope and peace. You'll need it.

TENTH LINK

Surrender Equals Peace

UNLINKED:

This anecdote is the only opposite. It is one of the experiences in my life where I worked the link. Unfortunately, I have had many, many days without peace, without surrender. Pushing for acting jobs, pushing for friendships, pushing for relationships, pushing for answers, pushing for control, always trying and doing, never allowing myself to just be.

This moment in time where I actually surrendered has stuck with me for years. It has become one of the markers in my world of chaos calling to me to find a consistently better way to live my life.

In the early nineties I traveled the country doing stand-up comedy. I specifically did a lot of college shows. Being in control and being funny are two main ingredients to having a successful show. This particular night I had neither.

Achieving Fulfillment

I am onstage in a huge auditorium in the deep south, contracted to perform for an hour and I am bombing horribly. 'Bombing' is the term one uses to describe doing the opposite of having the audience love you, cheer for you and laugh at every eyebrow twitch.

The room was predominantly dark except for the stage spot light so it was almost impossible to see individual faces in the crowd. When jokes or material doesn't go over well, I usually get them on my side by picking on people in the crowd especially at college shows. Not only was that not working it seemed to anger them even more.

They hated my material. They hated my clothes. I know because they told me so. They were out for blood and they were close to accomplishing their goal. In my experience I had dealt with some folks not loving me, but the amount of negativity coming from this crowd was unsurpassed. They were on their feet and not for a standing ovation. For some reason it didn't occur to me to run off stage. Maybe it did, but I knew I wanted to get paid. Suddenly I just stopped talking.

I stopped begging and cajoling. I stopped pleading and sucking up. I stopped insulting, berating and yelling and scolding. I shut up. They shut up. I kept breathing. Then out of this tornado of anxiety, fear, hatred and disgust I just started singing 'Amazing Grace'. As I said in the past I was not a religious person. I was backed in a corner hurt and confused because I just wanted to entertain them and make them laugh. Finally surrendering, not walking out or running away, but surrendering brought the crowd to its feet and gave us all the love we were looking for that night.

LINK:

Worry is cunning and deceitful. It makes you think you are actually accomplishing something besides driving yourself crazy and you are not.
Surrender is a magnificent ideal. You get to lay down all your armour and feel safe. You may have to surrender every single minute of every day but you know when you surrender you invite peace.

Surrender sounds like giving up and throwing in the towel. The difference is you are not ending the fight. The fight continues, you choose to release your strong hold on the outcome and enjoy the sparks.

Worry is like a rat in a maze that is in an endless circle. Self pity lets you wallow in all your bad decisions, laziness, ignorance and any other negative thing you have ever done or said. When you are tired of thinking these negative, harmful, sick making thoughts, the light of positive thinking and unselfish actions is always available to you. That is your surrender.

Surrender is like walking into the quiet room of your choice when you are so tired you can't even see straight and there before you is a large, clean comfortable bed that you can sleep in until you are fully rested and rejuvenated. *To surrender is to take everything and everyone that is part of your life, put them in a safe, healthy, happy place and then TRUST that everything will work out..THE WAY IT IS SUPPOSED TO.*

Achieving Fulfillment

Surrender means you trust you are doing ALL you can at the moment to help yourself. You trust that deep breaths and a clear head are better than tears and blame and self flagellation. Surrender. Turning your life over to that something greater (ninth link) will ease the stress on your body and calm the fear in your mind. Surrender is what you do when you are still taking action at the appropriate time. Surrender is what you do to keep living life on life's terms. Surrender is what you do to continue on your journey to fulfillment. You surrender, you are fulfilled.

Nothing takes the place of peace. Some of you know what life is like without it. Work these links. Ask for help when you need it. Surrender aloud or quietly even when you do not know to whom or what you are surrendering to. Keep your thoughts positive and in the present. Write things down when you feel confused or overwhelmed. Clean up thoughts and guilt from your past. Accept people, place and things as they are and stop thinking everyone is out to get you. Don't complain and do what works. Control yourself as well as speak up for yourself. Take care of your body and your mind. It is the only one you have. When you decide it is all about you and you are ready to achieve fulfillment, your experience on this earth will be better than you could ever imagine. Life is hard and not fair, but you can take it on as it comes. No worries. Always surrender. *Embrace every moment of peace.* You deserve it.

CONCLUSION

Picture these links as a buffet. You take what you like and leave the rest. Perhaps you sample a few items that are new to your palate. You may hate them; others you might find go down easier than expected. The point is that something in your life needs to change or at the least be amended.

The links do not have to be done in order. The way they are written seemed to be the logical progression but everyone is different. The goal is to be more at ease with yourself and your life, not to score 100% on your link usage. Working the ideas in this book give you carte blanche to be selfish. After all, if we are not right with ourselves how can we go into the world, greet our spouses, discipline our children, set boundaries in relationships, question our finances, or make empowering life decisions when we are behaving and thinking like hurt less than children? One more life anecdote from my illustrious past and I will let you go.

An old friend's birthday is one day before mine. Neither one of us had stellar social lives so we agreed to spend our birthdays together. At the time she lived about an hour and half away.

Achieving Fulfillment

I drove up the night before her birthday, spent the night and we had a fun celebration the next day. That night I stayed over looking forward to another fun day celebrating my birthday, but I was mistaken. Upon arising she informed me that she was just going to have some 'me' time today. No celebrating. Well thank you very much. I drove back to LA and had dinner alone.

I remained in touch with that 'friend' because obviously I felt that was how I should be treated. I visited one last time before she and her then fiance were set to move out of state. She asked me to come over because she said she had some clothes she wanted to give me. She also wanted relationship advice. She was having trouble deciding if she should marry her boyfriend or start dating the boyfriends best friend who was much cuter. Since I was single at the time, she loved to flaunt her two men in my lonely overworked face.

Arriving at her place to try on clothes that she gave me and then took back when I showed interest turned out to be a blessing. I was deep in the middle of trying to better my life. Trying to follow these links. Not sure if I was working on acceptance but I drove to her place expecting nothing but a change of scenery. I was open to the day and each of its moments.

That day I met my husband.

Yes, it turns out that the friend of the boyfriend saw her for what she was: someone who badly needed to practice these links! It was not a coincidence that I met my husband once I had decided to start treating myself better.

My "friend" did marry the boyfriend but they are no longer together. Not sure if they actually divorced but that is none of my business. We live in a different states now and obviously don't keep in touch. My husband and I have been in love since the day we independently and inadvertently showed up on that woman's door step. Synchronicity.

Since I was already in the process of cleaning up my emotional life I was thankfully available to the man I married. It is important to note here I was NOT cleaning up my life so I could get married. I never wanted to get married. The single life was more than fine, but making the changes in my life and trusting my gut lead me to a man I most certainly wanted by my side in theory and on paper.

Carl Jung, a Swiss psychiatrist, helped introduce us to the word 'synchronicity' meaning events that are "meaningful coincidences". We enjoy many meaningful coincidences in our lives but we are sometimes too wrapped up in our own negativity or worry to see them. These events can act as guideposts on our journey. Thinking about someone, seeing some things that reminds you of a friend (or foe) and you feel you should get in touch, mulling over finishing that book and all of a sudden emails and ads for publishing are before you (my experience), trying to decide where to move and suddenly you see bumper stickers and t-shirts from one particular place you considered suddenly appear, etc, etc are events that help guide you to do what it is you know you need to do for yourself.

This day happens to be a rainy day. I have been in NY now for over a year. The last few months I have been exhausting myself with auditions, working on my craft in my theatre group, rehearsing and performing with my improv group, assiduously watching movies as a juror for a prominent film festival, actively doing the basic housework, helping to care for my mother and trying to keep my marriage intact as we are still living in my mom's house. This rainy day marked the fourth week in a row that I would audition, get the callback, be placed on hold/first refusal and not book the job.

Donna Cooper

On a few hours sleep I dragged myself out of the callback to walk briskly in the rain, handing out advertisement cards for my theatre company. Though not in the show, my task was to deliver these cards to several prearranged locations. With every step, I grew sadder and more miserable than the minute before.

Completing my service I boarded a later train than expected and headed home balling like a neglected child. Ah, the past. I needed some comfort. Once I arrived home I got a call from a woman who wanted me to pay *her* a few thousand dollars to publish my book. This reminded me that 1. I was still in a holding pattern for securing a decent paying job and 2. I actually had not finished the last chapter of this book! And boy did I need to read it!

What we do, what we think and our perspective all help to create our lives, our reality. That higher power, that larger intelligence, is with us in creating. Keep exploring and learning and trying (and failing). Read and discuss things you agree with, disagree with and all that you don't understand. There is always something to learn to help ourselves in this world.

If all you get from this book is the ability to hear that voice inside, to trust your gut, then mission accomplished. It is easier to trust yourself when you get rid of old hurts, resentments and attitudes. These links are not guarantees, but they can be used as simple strategies to encourage and help you become more of an active participant in your life.

Use all the links. Use just one. Work them in order. Work them randomly. It really doesn't matter. If these links aren't for you try another book or tape or video. There is plenty of help out there.

Your best self and your best life is out there waiting.

Go get it.

Made in the USA
Coppell, TX
21 June 2022